Black Girls Gone Blonde: Stories From A Newly Discovered Sisterhood

Joani Ward

JOANI WARD

BLACK GIRLS GONE BLONDE

ISBN: 978-0-9960194-0-8 (Paperback edition)
ISBN: 978-0-9960194-1-5 (eBook edition)
ISBN: 978-0-9960194-2-2 (hardback edition)
Library of Congress Control Number: 2014943181

First Printing: 2014
Place of Publication: Washington, DC
Cover Design: William Maxwell – WM Graphics
Back Cover Photo: Maya Indigo
Makeup Artists: Brandi Nichole Dickerson/Noni Oseitutu

Acknowledgements

I express my deepest appreciation to the beautiful ladies that allowed me to enter their world through one-on-one interviews. They helped me to achieve this product; *Black Girls Gone Blonde: Stories From A Newly Discovered Sisterhood.* Our stories depict us as vulnerable, yet strong; determined, persistent, talented, emotional, loving, funny, inquisitive, dynamic, creative, intelligent and successful women. I feel a special bond with each of the ladies, and will be forever indebted to them for sharing their stories with me.

Table of Contents

Alphabets form words,
Words form sentences,
Sentences form thoughts,
Thoughts form paragraphs,
Paragraphs form pages,
Pages form chapters,
Chapters create books.

Introduction

I grew up listening to ad campaigns created for Clairol[1] by Shirley Polykoff[2] that included the following slogans, "If I've only one life to live, let me live it as a blonde" and "Is it true blondes have more fun." [3] Back then I had no intention or desire of becoming blonde, but I enjoyed the commercials. When I was a teenager I actually loved washing my hair with Herbal Essence Shampoo, a Clairol product.

Clairol

Clairol is a personal-care-product division of Procter & Gamble, which was created in 1931 by Lawrence and Joan Gelb, after discovering hair-coloring preparations while traveling in France.[4] The company was widely recognized in the United States for its "Miss Clairol" home hair-coloring kit, introduced in 1956. By 1959, Clairol was considered the leading company in the U.S. hair-coloring industry.

What was it about being a blonde that would make a woman change her natural hair color? Princess Diana spent almost 4,000£ ($6,284.80) a year to have her hair bleached.

Dr. Tony Fallone, an experimental psychologist, noted in 1997 that hair color is the root of a person's personality.[5]   In the Vogue Book of Blondes he says, "They are a special breed, especially dyed blondes.   Because blondes see and feel themselves as more glamorous, they project this, so others also see them this way. The thing about being blonde is that you are noticed more."[6]

Dr. Fallone further states "Blokes in vans turn round and look because you're blonde. So if you decide to go blonde you have to be ready to adjust to all the attention." Blondes are typically more outgoing and lively, and are perceived as more feminine than women with other hair colors. According to Dr. Fallone, being blonde is not a hair color, but a state of mind.

Clairol continued to market its hair color products with advertising slogans created by Mrs. Polykoff, who was also behind Clairol's campaign "Does she or doesn't she? Only her hairdresser knows for sure." This ad focused on whether a woman dyed her hair or not, and was inspired by Mrs. Polykoff's future mother-in-law. When the future mother-in-law met the future daughter-in-law she pulled her son to the side and inquired whether his girlfriend colored her hair. This slogan earned Mrs. Polykoff a place in the Advertising Hall of Fame.[7] It also became the eighth top advertising slogan of the 20th century.[8]

Mrs. Polykoff's advertising genius helped take Clairol's hair color revenue from $25 million to $200 million annually, with Clairol holding a 50% market share.[9] Even though her Clairol advertising campaign encouraged women to take charge of their own lives, she did not want to be seen earning more than her lawyer husband, and insisted that Foote, Cone and Belding (FCB), her advertising agency, cap her salary at

$25,000 a year. Upon the death of her husband, FCB immediately doubled her salary twice and promoted her.

According to some bean counters,[10] the number of women who suddenly became blondes shot up 413 percent due to the marketing campaigns of Mrs. Polykoff.[11] Does this 413 percent increase include any African-American women? I'm not sure, but I do wonder.

Clairol achieved notoriety in the late 1990s and early 2000s for its ads for Herbal Essence shampoo. The ads often featured women washing their hair and making sounds similar to those of someone having an orgasm.[12] Prior to the racier ads, Herbal Essence shampoo ads were cool, animated ads, depicting a woman in a colorful garden (similar to the Garden of Eden).[13]

In 2004, Clairol registered annual sales worth approximately $1.6 billion from the sale of its hair products.[14] Clairol currently manufactures hair-coloring products sold under the brand names "Natural Instincts," "Nice 'n Easy" and Age Defy."

Interesting Blonde Facts

While conducting research for my book, I uncovered some interesting Blonde Facts[15] which are found below.

Hydrogen peroxide was discovered in 1818[16], but there was little application for it until 1867, when it was found that it could bleach hair. It quickly became popular throughout Europe and America, superseding everything else that had been used as bleach before then.

Jean Harlow was Hollywood's first blonde goddess.[17] She dyed her hair with a mixture of peroxide, household bleach, soap flakes, and ammonia until it fell out and she was forced to wear a wig.

Blonde hair can range from practically white (platinum blonde) to a dark golden blonde. Strawberry blonde, the mixture of blonde and red hair, is the rarest type of blonde hair.

Let's fast forward to 2014. How does an African- American woman become blonde? Most of the women featured in my book become blonde the same way women did in the 1960's. We use a powdered lightener like BW2,[18] combined with a weighted developer, like Clairoxide[19] (10, 20, 30 or 40 weight). Using these products creates an array of blonde hues. The strength of the developer determines the magnitude of the lift.[20] Stylist probably use many techniques to achieve the blonde hues we black girls are rocking these days, but the technique I described is the one I'm most familiar with.

Research indicates that blondes are viewed as less intelligent than women with darker hair.[21] However, modern science shows that there is no evidence of intellectual differences based on hair color.

How about this? A Lithuanian firm called Olialia (ooh-la-la) announced in 2010 that it was going to build a resort in the Maldives that would employ only blonde women. It will also have a special airline staffed only by blondes that will take customers to the island. The resort is scheduled to open in 2015.

When I first devised the title for my book I wasn't sure of which spelling to use for "blonde." I learned the term "blonde" came from the French language and kept its masculine and feminine forms. Consequently, as a noun, "blond" is a fair-haired male, while "blonde" is a fair-haired female. However, when the word is used as an adjective, "blond" can be used for both males and females; however "blonde" can only be used to describe a woman or girl with fair hair.

The blonde stereotype has been divided into three categories: 1) the ice-cold blonde (Grace Kelley), 2) the blonde bombshell (Brigitte Bardot), and 3) the dumb blonde (Marilyn Monroe).

Scientists believe that blonde hair evolved in sun-deficient climates so that the body could synthesize vitamin D more efficiently. Other scholars, such as anthropologist Peter Forst, claimed blonde hair evolved very quickly as a means of sexual selection. The blonde hair and blue eyes of some northern European women made them more alluring to men.

Alfred Hitchcock, the "master of suspense," was obsessed with blondes, and almost exclusively cast blondes as his leading ladies.[22] His favorite blondes included Eve Marie Saint (*North by Northwest*), Joan Fontaine (*Suspicion*), Carol Lombard (*Mr. and Mrs. Smith*), Janet Leigh (*Psycho*), Grace Kelly (*Dial M for Murder, Rear Window*, and *To Catch a Thief*), and Tippi Hedren (*The Birds* and *Marni*). Scholars have noted that Hitchcock's blondes have become one of the most potent icons of our era.

Blonde hair is seen throughout fairy tales, including Rapunzel, Rumpelstiltskin, Cinderella, and Goldilocks. In fairytales, blonde hair often suggests strength, untarnished beauty, indestructibility, youth, and high value. In contrast, vice is associated with being hairy, dark, and ugly.

The Melanesians of New Guinea are the only dark-skinned group of humans in the world known to have naturally blonde hair.[23] They are an ethnic group from Melanesia, an island around Australia. Blonde hair is a trait that is seen naturally only in Europe, so how could these people, so far away, also have blonde hair?

It's based on the genetic makeup. Recent studies suggest that all humans outside of Africa have genes that have been passed down from Neanderthals, yet Melanesians are the only known humans whose prehistoric ancestors are slightly different, most likely the result of interbreeding with the Denisova hominin, a cousin of the Neanderthal. Because of this, they received slightly different genes, one of them being TYRP1,[24] which is unique to them and grants them blonde hair.

Naturally blonde hair is rare in humans, and found almost exclusively in Europe and Oceania, with TYRP1 being a major determinant of blonde hair in Solomon Islanders. [25]

Blonde Hair in the Workplace

There have been a number of employment discrimination cases involving Black women who have worn blonde hair. Here are a few you might find interesting:[26]

C. Santee v. Windsor Court Hotel

Burchette v. Abercrombie & Fitch

Bryant v. BEGIN Manage Program

Most recently, a story appeared in the Huffington Post[27] on October 22, 2013, regarding Farryn Johnson, a black woman in Baltimore who was fired from her job as a waitress at Hooters due to "improper image" after the 25-year-old refused to remove blonde highlights from her dark brown hair.

Ms. Johnson was told "Black women don't have blonde in their hair, so you need to take it out."

There were other employees working at the restaurant of other races with color in their hair. There were Asian girls with red hair and Caucasian girls with black hair and blond streaks, so Ms. Johnson didn't think it would be an issue for her to have the little piece of blond highlight in my hair.

Ms. Johnson has reportedly filed a racial discrimination complaint with the Maryland Commission on Civil Rights.

A Newly Discovered Sisterhood

What is sisterhood? Merriam-Webster.com defines sisterhood as the close relationship among women based on shared experiences, concerns, etc. It can also mean a community or society of women, such as a sorority, or community of nuns.

Dictionary.com defines sisterhood as an organization of women with a commonality, as   for social, charitable, business, or political purposes. Also defined as a congenial relationship or companionship among women; mutual female esteem, concern, support, etc.

I was going into a Starbucks in Rockville, MD one morning, prior to going to work. I encountered an African-American woman with a funky blonde haircut. We made eye contact and we each complimented one another on our hair. It wasn't just the compliment. It was the feeling I got when I received the compliment. A feeling of support or bonding, because we had each chosen to be different. We had each chosen to stand out. A totally appropriate quote for us by Dr. Seuss is:

"Why fit in when you were born to STAND OUT!"

As I approached other blonde, African-American women to write and submit stories for my book, I felt the same connection. I talked to hundreds of women who were very receptive to my book project, but just like people don't like to read, I guess most people also don't like to write.

21

The eight women that were brave enough to share their stories for this book are amazing. Their stories are true and very personal. The stories will make you smile, make you think, make you change, maybe even make you cry. The objective of the book is to convey the message that no matter what situation you're currently facing or have faced in the past, the situation can be changed to your advantage. You may not be able to see the light at the end of the tunnel right now, but it is there.

Joani Ward

Why am I blonde? I needed a change. I had to euthanize Fluffy, my West Highland Terrier, on May 14, 2012, and I was very sad. I made an appointment with my stylist and told her I needed a change to brighten my spirits. My stylist responded, "Let's go platinum."

The change in my hair color has made a noticeable difference. People seem friendlier and more receptive when I approach. I notice the gleam in men's eyes as I pass them or ask a question. And the connection I feel with other blonde African-American women is what prompted me to write Black Girls Gone Blonde: Stories From A Newly Discovered Sisterhood.

23

Now, my challenge is starting an organization, an actual community for beautiful, blonde African-American women to come together for social, charitable, and educational gatherings. I'm up for the challenge. Are you?

When sisters stand shoulder to shoulder, who stands a chance against us? ~Pam Brown

The Storyteller

As a business owner, I've been affiliated with several multi-level marketing (MLM)[28] companies. I've learned through this affiliation that facts tell, and stories sell. Most people don't want to hear a boat load of facts; they want to hear a story. And yes, I provided some facts in the introduction, but I found the information fascinating, and I wanted to share it. You either read the intro or you didn't, and that's okay. But I bet you learned some things if you did read it.

Anyway, I consider myself a pretty good storyteller, and the stories presented throughout the book are from the heart. The interviews conducted with the ladies were very intimate and personal. During the final stages of completing the book I created a Facebook page for Black Girls Gone Blonde. I received a comment from one of the women that liked my page that said "I found a home. Finally a community that embraces us."

And what do I say to that? I say Yes, a community that embraces us, a newly discovered sisterhood.

Growing Up

I was born in St. Louis, MO on January 10, 1957 at 5:57pm. I turned 57 this year, 2014. On my birthday I kept telling my family and friends they needed to play combinations of my birthday because 57 was so prominent in the way the numbers were falling. Not sure if anyone did.

I'm the first born to William Sr. (deceased) and Zora Anita Ward. Two brothers followed me, William Jr. (Bill) and Kelvin Sr. We had a very happy childhood. No complaints. My Mom and Dad always instilled in us excellent work ethics. I admired my parents because they worked together as a great team. They worked hard, pooled their earnings, paid their bills and made a great life for my brothers and me.

I attended Cupples and Yeatman Elementary Schools, and Northwest High School. I had two best friends, Deborah Stewart (now Deborah Miller) and Cheryl Benbow (now Cheryl Thomas). We were inseparable. I miss those summer nights sitting on the porch talking about girl stuff. You know, the boys we had a crush on, going shopping, or just sitting there saying nothing. The mere presence of Debbie and Cheryl was enough for me.

I remember the little things, like the day I started my menstrual cycle. I was 13 years old, outside playing. I had on pink and white seersucker shorts. My Mom called me in the house to talk. This was my moment, the beginning of cramps from Hell!!! I can laugh about it now since I don't have those menstrual cycles anymore-hysterectomy in 2000.

I left St. Louis in 1975 to attend Howard University. I studied at Howard for 2 years; started with Political Science and hated it. Changed to the School of Communications and hated it. Wanted to major in Business Management, but was intimidated with math.

This is so ironic because now I'm an Adjunct Professor teaching classes such as Financial Decision Making, Managerial Accounting and Quantitative Methods.

It took me a while to get my act together, but I completed my undergraduate studies at George Washington University – Mount Vernon Campus (1991) and received my MBA from The Johns Hopkins University – Carey Business School (2001).

I worked for a wonderful company for 27 years and gained a wealth of knowledge regarding the financial industry. I retired from the 9-5 world on January 31, 2014, and I'm still adjusting. I'm a business owner, so I still wakeup early, seem to be busier now than I was when I worked 9-5 and ran a business, and stay up till the wee hours of the morning because I'm so wound up with creating a prosperous and sustainable business.

I know I should go to bed earlier, but as an entrepreneur I'm always researching, finding ways to make my business better, finding ways to make myself better, finding ways to help others achieve business success. Probably why I can't lose weight, not enough sleep.

My Favorite Christmas

As I mentioned earlier, my parents made a great life for my brothers and me. Christmas at my house was always a very special time of the year. My brother Bill and I got everything we wanted for Christmas. The excitement on Christmas Eve and waiting for Santa was almost unbearable. We would wake our parent's at the crack of dawn, so we could open our gifts.

Here's a snapshot of what I remember – talking toys like Bugs Bunny, Linus the Lion, and Cecil the Dragon, tricycles, bicycles with training wheels, 10-speed bikes, Mrs. Beasley and other dolls, play guns with holsters and rifles, cowboy hats, Tinkertoy Construction Sets, board games like Go To The Head of the Class, Monopoly, Sorry, and Operation, televisions, clothing, shoes, sneakers, money. You name it, we got it.

Eventually Bill and I stopped believing in Santa Claus, but Kelvin, my youngest brother, still got excited at the thought of Santa bringing everything on his Christmas list. So, the excitement of Christmas and Santa Claus lived on for a little while longer.

With Kelvin being the major gift receiver now, the Christmas Eve ritual was to make sure Kelvin was asleep, gather in the dining room to wrap all the gifts around 10:00pm, and put them under the tree. This was such a fun time. Imagining what Kelvin's reaction would be with each gift he opened made me very happy. One of his favorite gifts was a drum set. He loved drums, and he could really play them. It was like he was born to play. I remember he received drums on at least two Christmases because he beat a hole in the snare. Wouldn't you know it. When Kelvin got old enough, he went on to play the drums with the Santa Clara Vanguard Drum and Bugle Corps.[29]

One Christmas season, probably during 1968 or 1969, my Mom and I were out shopping for gifts. We passed a watch counter and I caught a glimpse of a navy blue watch. Blue is my favorite color. The watch had a navy blue band and navy blue face, with silver accents for the bezel and numbers. It was a Timex. I summoned my Mom to the watch counter and mentioned that it was a nice watch. She agreed.

On Christmas Eve my Mom and I assembled in the dining room to wrap gifts for Kelvin, Bill and Daddy. We talked about different things and anticipated everyone's excitement when they opened their gifts on Christmas morning. I left the dining room for a moment, and when I returned, my Mom handed me a box that she had wrapped. She said, "Merry Christmas, Precious." I had no idea what was in the box. I unwrapped it and found the blue Timex watch that I had fallen in love with. I was speechless and overwhelmed with emotion. I was so happy that all I could do was cry.

I mentioned earlier, Christmas was always a very special time in my house, but in comparison, the Christmas I received the blue Timex watch from my Mom was my favorite Christmas.

Heading To College

In August 1975 I left St. Louis heading to Washington, DC to attend Howard University. I was excited about my new independence, and thought my brothers would be glad I was gone; so they could take over my room. Bill never really mentioned how he felt about me leaving for school, but in 2011 Kelvin shared something very special with me.

We were texting. Kelvin told me "something about the sky reminded him of the day I left St. Louis. Something about the grayness of the day brought about the same sad feelings he felt when I left for Howard University."

I was excited about the new friendships I was going to make. Kelvin was sad that his big sister wouldn't be home when he finished baseball practice. I was excited about exploring a new city. Kelvin was probably wondering why I never asked to speak to him when I called home. I was excited about being on my own. How could I not be tuned into my little brother's feelings?

Kelvin and I were very close, even though there is a ten-year difference in our ages. He followed me everywhere when we were younger. He even remembers that his first visit to McDonald's was with me. It never dawned on me that Kelvin was sad I was gone, and it broke my heart when he shared this sadness with me.

The moral of this story, don't get so tied up in yourself and what you're doing that you forget to pay attention to the people that love you. Fortunately, Kelvin and I are closer now than we were when we were younger. There's nothing like a brother's love.

Love Is....

My Dad died from prostate cancer in May 2007. During 2007 his health started to deteriorate rapidly. Watching this was very difficult for me. I hated hearing the phone ring because I always thought it might be my Mom calling to tell me my Dad was gone. I became distant and irritable.

I flew home to St. Louis as often as I could; Christmas, Valentine's Day, and for my Dad's birthday, March 18th. My Dad got weaker every visit. He was confined to the bed when I went home in March for his birthday. Family and friends gathered around his bed to sing happy birthday and read his cards to him. My turn came, and I was holding the card from my Mom. I started to read it:

Because I Love You So Much

Just in case there is any kindness I can show you,
Just in case there is something special I can do,
Just in case there is any dream I can help you fulfill,
I will do those things.

Just in case you don't see it in my smile,
Just in case you don't feel it in my touch,
Just in case you don't hear it every time I speak your name,
I love you now, and forever.

There was more to the card, but this was as far as I could read. I got choked up and passed the card to Kellie, my niece, to finish. Let me explain why. My Dad and Mom loved each other very much, but it often seemed that my Dad got on my Mom's nerves. He was a real talker and joker. My Mom, on the other hand was more serious.

Now, here's the catch. My Mom puts a lot of thought into the greeting cards she gives, so I knew the card I was holding was from her heart. Reading the card made me realize just how much my Mom loved my Dad, and I became overwhelmed.

This visit was the last time I saw my Dad. He transitioned on May 3, 2007, and my Mom was by his side when he took his last breath.

Something very special I remember about my Dad was he loved to sing, and he sang love songs to my Mom. One of his favorite songs, written by Ray Noble and sung by Nat King Cole was "The Very Thought Of You."

The Very Thought Of You, written by Ray Noble

The very thought of you, and I forget to do,
The little ordinary things that everyone ought to do.
I'm living in a kind of daydream,
I'm happy as a king.
And foolish though it may seem, to me that's everything.

The mere idea of you, the longing here for you,
You'll never know how slow the moments go, till I'm near to you.
I see your face in every flower, your eyes in stars above,
It's just the thought of you, the very thought of you, my love.

Laws of Attraction – The Tuxedo

Summer 2012 I made plans to attend a formal affair and wanted to wear a Donna Karan tuxedo. I knew the tuxedo was going to be pricey. I thought about the tuxedo every day, but I kept putting off the purchase. The Sunday before my event I attended church services at Unity of Washington, DC,[30] and the tuxedo was heavy on my mind. My intent was to go to Pentagon City Mall[31] after church to see if I could find my Donna Karan tuxedo. After church, I was walking to my car. I was parked on a side street, and when I turned the corner from 13th Street NW I saw a tuxedo hanging on the fence. I initially kept walking, but something told me to go back and look at the tuxedo. The tuxedo was from Joseph A. Banks. There was a sign on the fence that said something like "take these if you need them." There was also a box full of shoes under the tuxedo. I took the tuxedo, came home, tried it on, and to my amazement, it fit. Just goes to show that what you think about, you bring about.

What's In Store

I retired from the 9-5 world on January 31, 2014. I'm still getting used to this new world. Seems I'm busier now developing my consulting business, writing books, networking, going to the gym to get my body right, and everything else that comes up than when I was working 9-5.

So, what's in store? I'm going to travel to the places I've always wanted to visit. I want to see the Great Pyramid of Giza, Stonehenge, the Taj Mahal, the Coliseum in Rome, and Aurora Borealis. I want to stay at The Manta Resort (Pemba Island, Zanzibar), Africa's first underwater hotel and the Ice Hotel (Northern Sweden), a hotel made entirely from ice and snow. Take a safari to Tanzania's Serengeti and a gondola ride in Venice, Italy. Have afternoon tea at Fortnum and Mason[32] in Piccadilly, London and watch Serena Williams play tennis at Wimbledon.

I'll continue writing books, hosting seminars and webinars, and helping others create sustainable businesses from their passions. My greatest passion is to provide financial literacy for children. When I was growing up, the conversation at dinner time didn't focus on investing in the stock market, income producing assets, entrepreneurship, or wealth creation. We were consumers. I often wonder how different my life may have been if I had read Rich Dad Poor Dad when I was in high school. But I've also heard things happen in Devine time.

I'm grateful for all my challenges; they've made me a stronger person. I'm grateful for all my successes; they keep me confident and help me understand I have to help others achieve their success.

My Newly Discovered Sisterhood

The ladies you are about to meet are beautiful, brilliant, bold, intelligent, funny, witty, sexy, tall, short, and athletic. I could go on and on, but I'll let you discover the many traits and characteristic held by each of the ladies. You'll learn the challenges they've encountered and how they overcame them. You'll see how talented they are and experience their successes.

My newly discovered sisterhood consists of Santa, Katrina, Brittany, Frankie, J., Candice, Antoinette, and Brandi. This is a brave bunch of ladies. I approached hundreds of women during my search for stories for the book, and these are the brave souls that came to my rescue. I have to also give special thanks to Santa, because she also recruited ladies to share their stories. The book would never have come to fruition without this special group of ladies. So, I thank them with all my heart. They are the perfect verse over a tight beat.

Santa Leah Jones

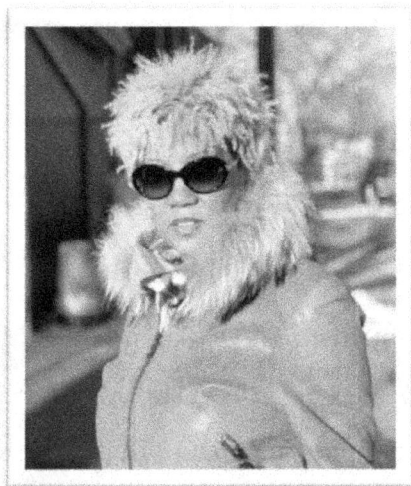

Santa Leah Jones has been blonde since late 1970, when she played the lead role in a play called ***Mae's Rent Party***. Santa says, "You must have a certain attitude that goes with the various shades, and for me the lighter the better. Blondes generally have a strong air of confidence. I stand apart and make a statement: check me out!! To me, being blonde means knowing yourself and truly liking what you've become. The brighter my hair, the happier I feel!"

41

Prayers Come True

Santa was the first person I interviewed for the book. We met on the morning of Feb. 9, 2013. I've known Santa for years. We would run into each other occasionally at parties, and were always cordial, but never really became close friends. So, I didn't really "know" Santa.

During summer 2012 I ran into Santa at the William H. Rumsey Aquatic Center[33] at Eastern Market,[34] in Washington, DC. I told her about my project to write Black Girls Gone Blonde, and she was totally receptive.

During our time together Santa and I discussed several issues. I wanted to know how she was feeling, more about her background, and I wanted Santa to share a segment of her life that would inspire others. I asked Santa a series of questions, and her responses follow.

The first question I asked was "how are you feeling?" Santa was in a great mood; very positive. She was feeling fabulous. Santa felt the interview was a blessing, and it meant a lot to her. She was also honored to be my first interviewee; she was happy.

Growing Up

I wanted to delve into Santa's background and learned that she is a Washingtonian who grew up on the northeast (NE) side of Capitol Hill. In 1975, Santa's Mother wasn't able to purchase the house they were living in; the landlord was interested in selling his house and presented an offer to Santa's Mother. Santa's Mother couldn't afford to buy the house because she wasn't working, was on welfare, and was raising 9 children. Santa, born in 1961, was 13 years old when this happened. The family moved to public housing in 1975 on the southeast (SE) side of Washington, DC. To be more specific, they moved to Potomac Gardens.[35]

Santa described public housing as a different type of atmosphere; and she didn't like it. She originally lived in a 3 bedroom row house, so transitioning to public housing was difficult.

Santa witnessed a lot of drug use, filthy apartments, and congested hallways. There were instances where you had to say excuse me for 10 minutes before you could get in your home. The media was always on the property. There was constant fighting, and Santa prayed continuously that she would get out of public housing. When she grew up she wanted a different life.

Santa was a tough cookie, so she didn't have any problems with people bothering or bullying her when she was living in Potomac Gardens. People actually wanted to be her friend because she was respectful and nice. She did her.

Santa attended Golden Elementary School and Stuart Jr. High when she and her family lived in the row house. She attended Dunbar after the move. A problem kid in school; she stayed in trouble.

Making It Out Of the Hood

Santa lived in Potomac Gardens from the time she was 13 years old to her early 20s. She eventually found her own place, and made sure it wasn't Section 8. **She got out**.

It was very important to Santa that she pay market rate rent. She found her own one bedroom apartment. Santia, Santa's daughter, went to school with all the other kids in the neighborhood. Santa wanted to show her daughter something different. When her lease was up she moved into a more diverse neighborhood, Cleveland Park.[36] Santa made sure Santia's upbringing was totally different from the way she was raised. According to Santa, "there is a way out, regardless the situation. You don't have to be stuck here. It's all about choices."

Prayers Do Come True

The day Santa found her house was truly a blessing. When she lived in public housing, she frequented a corner store one block away from Potomac Gardens. There was a little house across the street from the store, where an older guy lived. He always had his first floor lit up.

45

There was just something intriguing about his home. As Santa walked down the street she would look at the house, pray and say "when I move out of Potomac Gardens, all I need is a house like that." She kept praying as the years went by. When she got tired of renting, she looked through the newspaper and found a house for sale that she liked. She didn't realize this was the same house she had prayed on.

When Santa lived in public housing she knew how to get to work and school, but didn't have a sense of direction regarding the location of the house she had prayed on for so long. She also didn't pay attention to the numbers on the houses. The ad in the newspaper read 909 12th Street SE. Santa called the number and spoke with the agent. When she was on her way to see the property, she got to 12th Street and Pennsylvania Avenue, but it still didn't dawn on her that she was on her way to the house that she had prayed for. Santa was just saying, "OMG this is by Potomac Gardens." She burst into tears when she crossed I Street because she knew God had answered her prayers.

Santa has lived in her perfect house for 20 years, and has used her interior design expertise to turn it into a home worthy of appearing in the Metro Weekly[37] magazine. She is the sole proprietor of 909 Design.

A Happy and Healthy Life

Santa's daughter, grand kids and partner make her extremely happy. It's a blessing to see her grand kids growing up. It's a blessing to see that her daughter is a good Mom and wife, and that she has a thriving business. It's a blessing that Santa's partner brings tons of joy into her life.

Santa and her wife, a beautiful, phenomenal woman, have been together 11 years. Opposites attract. Where her wife is weak, Santa is strong, and vice versa. They're good for one another. They met on Oct. 9, 2003. Communication makes the relationship work; the key to any relationship. So, Santa and her wife are best friends, sisters, and lovers. They like to travel, eat well and exercise. They've travelled to Europe, Martha's Vineyard and Punta Cana.

Santa believes in taking care of her body, so she is adamant about eating well. She has incorporated lots of fresh vegetables into breakfast. Steams spinach and asparagus. Only eats egg whites. For exercise, Santa does deep water walking at the William H. Rumsey Aquatic Center and yoga.

Santa feels extremely good about where she is today in her life compared to where she came from. She is a strong advocate of prayer, and believes anything you want to accomplish; you can. Just stay focused and pray. Even if you don't see the staircase, just take the first step. You can make it.

Santa's Mom

As our interview came to a close, I asked Santa to describe a situation that really upset her. Here's what she shared with me.

On one of Santa's visits to see her Mom in the hospital, her Mom asked Santa to sit and not to leave her. Her Mom was crying and was in extreme pain; calling on the Lord, saying she was ready to go on home with Him because she was tired. Santa told her Mom she didn't know what to do. Her Mom told her she couldn't do anything.

"Don't leave me!" her Mom said. Santa could remember it like it was yesterday; rubbing her Mom's hair until she fell asleep, and praying for her to go on with the Lord. She was in so much pain, and was ready to go.

Santa talked to her Mom on a regular basis.

MOM

You have been such an inspiration to me.
I love the way you molded me.
I've always listened to the things you told me.
I've let my tears dry up with happy memories.
You have taken your journey to heaven where your new
life begins.
I will miss you profusely.

Katrina Roye

As I was getting out of high school, I was so tired of the dark Gotham colored hair I had. I knew my Mother and Father would say something, but getting a little older, I knew it wouldn't matter anymore. I started simple, not drastic. No reds, greens, or oranges, lol.[38] I decided to go light brown. I graduated with that color, and realized it brought out a lot of what I thought was a plain Jane face. So, that's when I decided to go lighter, which would be a golden blonde. I was so excited and pressed to get it done, that I decided to perm my hair first. I know the fine print clearly warns to wait at least 10 days to color hair after chemical usage, but know what? I still colored my hair, thinking it can take it because my hair is so thick and coarse. As I'm waiting for the finishing results, my scalp began to tingle. So when I take the cap off, I look like Tina Turner in "What's Love Got To Do With It." My edges came out, the middle of my hair came out, and my scalp was patchy and sore. My color was amazing. After the hollering and crying, and listening to my Mom say "I told you so" I looked in the mirror, laughed, and said "I got my blonde, and it looks good!!"

Moving Forward

I met Katrina on Feb. 9, 2013, and she's a beauty. She was 28 years old when we met. We talked as though we had known each other for years. We touched on her life concerns, family challenges and her passions. During our conversation I felt like I was listening to the younger sister I never had. I wondered why Katrina was able to be so open with me during our conversation. She told me she felt it was time to let her story out. Katrina looked at this as her therapy.

Don't Judge

Katrina has a deep concern for the way we, as humans, see one another. She used the term "understanding" as she explained her feelings. Katrina's exact words were, "understanding is a big thing, and I think our world doesn't see when we look at each other. We see the outer image, so we judge. We see the clothes, the hair, tattoos, jewelry. We assume this is the person, not knowing there was a past. They may not be that person that you just assume them to be. That's what I want the world to know. Everyone has a past, and everyone has their own opinions. Their opinions are an expression of where they came from, and what they know. Having an open mind to understand that is important and makes sense."

When Katrina was 15 years old she got a snake tattoo. Matter of fact, she had a snake. Now Katrina has numerous tattoos which focus on various expressions of temptation, and where she is in her life. Her tattoos include depictions of drugs, music, alcohol, Eve the Temptress, Money, Dead Bodies, Peace, and Black Power. Everyone wants power, and power comes in many forms.

Katrina's temptation stems from being promiscuous. Not knowing how to say No. Always accommodating. Always saying Yes. Wanting to be the in person; wanting to be in the in crowd.

When Katrina was younger, she got teased a lot about the way she dressed. She and her siblings didn't have the clothes that other kids had. They didn't get the new kicks that everyone else had. So they went to school wearing hand me downs. Grandmother and other family members tried to help. Judgments and expressions were made that Katrina's clothes were "grannies" clothes and she was making them into her own fashion. She was just trying to fit in. She wanted to be a part of something, but people were busy making judgments, not knowing Katrina's story.

Growing Up

Katrina grew up in NE Washington, DC. 21st and Trinidad. She attended every school on the hill, Charles Young Elementary, Brown Junior High School and Spingarn High School. That was pretty much her area. After junior high school, Katrina attended Margaret Murray Washington School[39] (MM Washington School) for a year. She wanted to be a nurse. MM Washington School wasn't a good fit for Katrina;

too many girls, too crowded and the students had pompous attitudes.

After her experience at MM Washington School, Katrina decided she didn't want to be a nurse anymore. She explained, "She's seen a lot." We all know that your insurance or your income determines how you're treated, if you get sick, and Katrina saw this in action. Medicaid[40] and Medicare[41] predict what type of medicine the doctor prescribes, and how you're treated. This is the total opposite of why Katrina wanted to be a nurse. She wanted to help, heal and treat people. She also learned there is a real distinction between PPO[42] and Medicaid.

Run and Hide

Katrina's Father was in the military, a Marine, and served in the Vietnam War. He was 10 years her Mother's grace. Serena, Katrina's older sister, was 2 years old when her Father and Mother met.

Her Father started doing drugs while he was in the military, and was addicted to heroin.

Katrina's Mother started doing drugs when she met Katrina's Father, and was addicted to crack. Katrina thinks her Mom started doing drugs to cope with her situation.

Katrina's Mom was 34 years old with 5 kids. By Katrina being the middle child, she helped out a lot; took on a lot regarding the household. Raising 5 kids can be overwhelming.

Katrina's parents would take gifts and money that was supposed to be for the kids and sell them for drugs. Kids never got the gifts. Relatives couldn't understand why the kids never called to thank them for the gifts and money. Katrina's Father even unwrapped Christmas gifts and sold them for money to buy drugs.

Dudes Katrina was talking to as a teenager were selling her Mother drugs. It was embarrassing, but common in the neighborhood.

Katrina's Mom would leave and not come home. Her Father would have hysterical fits because he didn't know where his wife was. Katrina would fend for her siblings. Her mother referred to Katrina as "her little soldier."

One night, Katrina was awakened by Serena screaming. Katrina caught her Father on top of Serena; molesting her. He didn't penetrate Serena, but still molestation. Katrina recalled that it was almost like her Father didn't realize what he was doing. He was drunk and high. He kept saying "I'm so sorry." Katrina started crying, and Serena continued screaming and crying.

The next day the situation was brushed under the rug. Katrina remembered her Father coming home from work, giving them money and apologizing. The following Sunday the family went to church. Serena told the Sunday school teacher what her Father had done. A week later Child Protection Services[43] (CPS) came to get the children. Serena's friend Nicole told Katrina she needed to run and hide because the people were coming to take her; detective style car. Katrina, her younger twin sisters, Valencia and Sonia, and Serena were taken into a foster care home on Alabama Avenue SE. She kept asking, "Where's my Mom?" CPS asked Katrina what happened, and she told them. Katrina's younger brother, Wesley, was in the hospital at this time, due to having been in a car accident, and wasn't taken into foster care.

Months passed, and they were literally around the corner from their house. The lady, Ms. Brooks, was nice, church going, and made dresses. Katrina was 8, Valencia and Sonia were 3. She fended for her sisters. They didn't know what was going on. The twins went home first. Katrina wanted to go home, but Serena didn't. Serena went into the system.

Happily, Katrina finally went back home. She loves her parents and knew her Father was sorry for what he had done. She also understands why Serena didn't want to go home.

Katrina has been the big sister in the household since the incident; making sure her

Mom and siblings were taken care of. Mother and Father were still together and still using drugs. They were functioning addicts.

The Aftermath

Katrina's Mom was bitter because she wanted Serena to come back home. Her Mom tried to cover what happened. No one wants to have a child that feels like they're a victim. Katrina's parents had been together for a long time, and the marriage was her Mother's everything. She wanted to mend the problem, but it couldn't be mended fast. It takes time for wounds like this to heal. Everyone had separate counseling, but they really needed group counseling. Crazy emotions come from your past; things you brushed under the rug. Katrina believes she wouldn't be able to erase the lingering emotions, had she been molested by her Father.

A Passion For Dance

Her past, experiencing certain things, required a mindset change. Katrina passionately wanted to be a dancer, but didn't have any support from her family. Instead of being focused on her passion, she was worried about trying to get by; finishing school, getting a job to put food on the table for her siblings, and support the family. Her passion for dance causes her to get emotional when she sees dancers on television. Says to herself "that could have been me."

Katrina often wants to tell her Mother it's her fault that she wasn't able to experience becoming a successful dancer. She refrains. She thinks "You didn't give me these things, you didn't help me with these things." But Katrina knew her Mother had a past. Her Grandmother suffered from mental illness. There are issues that her Mom dealt with that caused her actions in adult life. Katrina's Grandmother did the best she could raising her Mom and her Mom's siblings, but it was the bare minimum. Food on the table, a roof over their head. She wasn't able to tell them I love you, nor did she have time to do things a mother would do.

It Takes A Village

Katrina's paternal Grandmother taught her the girly things she needed to know. There's no excuse for her Father's actions as an adult. He came from a privileged family. Fair skin, pretty hair, money, cars. Katrina learned a lot from her paternal Grandmother. She acquired an expensive taste for good food and clothes. Grandmother instilled the little things that are important about hygiene, making your bed, little girly things. It takes a village to raise a child – her paternal Grandmother.

God put people in their lives to make sure they were ok. Church made sure they went on trips. Teachers knew their parents couldn't afford much. Fifth grade teacher went to school with Katrina's Father and Aunt. The teacher paid for Katrina to go on a field trip to Kings Dominion. A lady from church took the twins under her wing. Made sure they had school clothes and other necessities. The teacher knew Valencia and Sonia had an older sister working at CVS, trying to help support the family. So it was a big help that someone else was able to do the things Katrina wasn't able to, due to work obligations.

The Siblings

Katrina's siblings look at her as the mother. Her opinion counts. She was stern and didn't always tell her siblings yes. Didn't want her siblings to go through the things she went through like selling her body, doing drugs, and selling drugs to get by – putting food on the table. She thanks God that she is alive and breathing, walking. 28 and no kids.

Wesley, is unique. He's 21 now. He is a good boy, doesn't do any drugs. The only bad thing Katrina could think of regarding her brother was that he threw rocks at Ms. Pauline's house when he was 5 years old.

Wesley may have erased some of the things he saw when he was younger. Certain things he put a blind over, like seeing his Mom do drugs. He's just an amazing young man, considering he wasn't raised by his Father. His Father wasn't in the household; didn't teach him to play football. Mother taught him to play football. Father and son are currently building a relationship with each other.

Katrina always encourages Wesley to do everything he can. He's just doing so well, especially in the times we're living in. During the time he was growing up, and the environment he grew up in, you would think he would have ended up on the streets, hustling drugs, out there trying to get that new pair of shoes. He's not even into that. He was more into sports. Just being him, a leader more so than a follower. So, their relationship is very close. He is Katrina's baby. He's her everything. She would do anything for that little boy. And it's just because he's doing everything for himself. Katrina just wants to make sure he's okay, and doesn't fall through the cracks.

Valencia and Sonia are also doing excellent. Valencia works at the same Whole Foods as Katrina, in the floral department. Sonya just completed the work toward her bachelor's degree in Criminal Justice, and has started working. A lot of the past they don't know. They know of it, but the family doesn't talk about it. They didn't witness it like Katrina. So they didn't grow up with the incident weighing on them. They didn't grow up with the close relationship with their Father. They grew up fast. Smoking weed and drinking when they were 15. Katrina pushed them to get out of school – finish. Told them this is the easiest thing to do. They look up to Katrina, so she is constantly checking herself to make sure she's projecting the right image. Now Valencia and Sonia are focused and responsible. They understand that life is more than getting high, drinking, and having guys. Life is about learning, adventure, doing things you want to do, and being about something. Not letting your past hold you back, and keeping you from doing the things you want to do.

Natural Wellness and Homeopathic Care

Katrina's new passion is working in natural wellness, homeopathic care, body care. She helps people on a daily basis. People come back and tell her how great something has worked for them. According to Katrina, "Natural health care is like a hidden secret. If the FDA isn't approving, promoting or licensing something, people are hesitant to want or use it. People question why this big agency doesn't want to license this?"

Moving forward, Katrina sees a career in Nutritional Wellness. She wants to motivate people and open their awareness to natural healthcare. There's a business owner in the future – Katrina went to school for massage therapy. That's what really opened her mind to having her own business. She was fascinated while in school learning about the herbs and nutrition, and how they interact with the human body.

Katrina was looking for employment doing massage therapy. She was promoting her services, but money wasn't consistent, and that's what she needed. She was working with a nutritionist who shopped at Whole Foods. One day Katrina and her friend went to Whole Foods and Katrina was attracted to the way everyone genuinely seemed to like their jobs. She immediately felt this was where she needed to be. She had retail experience; didn't need a degree to get in. Katrina filled out the application and started as a cashier at Whole Foods. She wanted to be in Whole Body, so she started networking with people at Whole Foods, and built up her resume.

Katrina met Ahene Brown, a buyer at Whole Foods, and they talked. Ahene had long beautiful locks down to her butt, and she was pregnant. Katrina thought Ahene was beautiful. From then on they became great acquaintances. As they talked, Katrina found out Ahene was also a massage therapist. Kindred spirits. Ahene told Katrina whenever a spot opened in Whole Body, they would move her over. Ahene was moving into a managerial position, so she told Katrina, she could get Katrina in the door.

Katrina was able to transfer from Customer Service (after being there for 6 months) to Whole Body, and she's been there ever since. Associate Team Leader for Whole Body. Been at Whole Foods for 6 years. Started at 14th and P and moved to the Foggy Bottom store, near GW Hospital. The Universe opened up when Katrina needed it to.

If it wasn't for Whole Foods, Katrina doesn't know where she would be now, just in terms of living. (She got very emotional talking about this.) "I would say providing for myself. It's bigger than just providing for yourself financially. Emotionally and mentally." Katrina learns something new every day at Whole Foods, and she takes that knowledge back to her family and friends.

Brighter Days

Katrina's final message was that you don't have to be a product of your environment. She doesn't want to be dependent on Section 8 and Welfare. Her Mom was handicapped with

Welfare and Section 8. You don't have to be codependent on anything or anybody. Katrina looks forward to brighter days and a rewarding future as a business owner.

Brittany Bradford

Brittany first became blonde when she was 16, a sophomore in high school. She did because her mother said blondes have more fun, and she thought she could use more excitiement in her life. So my question to Brittany was "Do you actually have more fun?" Her response was "I guess so, yeah." As Brittany and I talked, I learned her friends think she looks better with blonde hair, she attracts more attention with blonde hair, and she loves attention.

69

Fashion Designing Lawyer in the Making

I met Brittany on February 16, 2013. She was the youngest of my interviewees, 18 years old. Sitting in her kitchen, I had the pleasure of meeting Brittany's Mom while we had coffee.

I was first introduced to Brittany via a picture. She had a blonde bush. Brittany's natural hair color is brown. Since taking that picture, Brittany has cut her hair, been bald, blonde again, almost platinum, then she got braids. She loves changing her hair.

Brittany has a brother, but they are 17 years apart. She was born in DC, but has lived in Virginia most of her life. She and her Mom are pretty close; best friends.

Brittany attended Washington Lee High School[44] on North Stafford Street in Arlington, VA. She told me she only likes school sometimes. Once she became a junior she just liked school less and less. Brittany wanted high school to be over. She wants to go to college to become a lawyer.

Brittany either wants to go to the University of Maryland, Spelman, or NYU to major in law or criminal justice, and minor in fashion design or forensics. She wants to be a lawyer because she used to be in the court system. She watched lawyers that didn't do their jobs well. Wants to be a juvenile lawyer for kids under the age of 18, because she watched how lawyers don't even care and don't pay attention to what really happened. Brittany stated "Lawyers will make a decision just based on how they feel, and she thinks that's really unfair. I feel like I can be someone's lawyer and really help them, and not just make money."

The Clothing Line

Brittany is currently working on a clothing line, and suggested creating a line for Black Girls Gone Blonde. She has a logo for her clothing line; BWare – a lion with blonde hair. Has designs. Knows someone that has a clothing line called Robotic Minds[45] – super stars are wearing it. Wants her line to be equally successful. She's very talented.

About Brittany

Brittany loves to party, loves mirrors, and loves photo shoots. Didn't answer her phone when I called the morning of our interview, so I thought she had been out partying. She went to bed at 1am. Brittany likes getting dressed up and looking nice. Likes it a lot. Believes a made face creates you.

Brittany was molested when she was younger. Had a problem letting people or situations go. Prior relationship helped her because she was able to communicate her feelings about the molestation. Helped her get over it. Having a good support system was very important.

Brittany likes helping others. She worked with a group called Lose the Training Wheels,[46] volunteering to help children with special needs learn to ride bikes. This was a great experience.

We take for granted learning to ride a bike. It took a week to teach the kids to ride the bikes. She thinks kids with special needs have really big hearts. I told Brittany about my experience tutoring homeless children, and the little girl that told me she wanted to kill herself because she hated being homeless. Brittany saw a homeless man and asked her Mom if they could get him a blanket and make him breakfast. They did it.

Her tongue is pierced, and she has Listen tattooed on her finger – a reminder to listen; Dreamcatcher on her ribcage, Love is Pain under her breast.

Hanging Out

On March 17th I had the opportunity to hang out with Brittany. She volunteered to create a t-shirt design for Black Girls Gone Blonde, so we went shopping for the raw materials; t-shirts, dye, rubber bands, and fabric scissors. The navigation system in my Lexus took us all over the world trying to find a Dollar Store. We ended up at Target, and were able to find t-shirts. Went to several other stores but couldn't find any Rit dye or rubber bands. This was a Sunday, so the stores were closing around 6pm. I told Brittany I would purchase the remaining products from Michaels.

While we were in route to the Dollar Store Brittany mentioned a pizza place, Jumbo Slice Pizza in Adams Morgan[47] that had really good pizza. We stopped by Jumbo Slice. When the owner of this establishment chose the name, he wasn't joking. One slice of pizza was as large as a whole pizza. I couldn't believe my eyes.

This was a great day with Brittany. Yet another occasion where I felt that sisterly bond.

Loving Life

As our interview came to a close I asked Brittany what she wanted the world to know about her. Here's what she shared. "I want the world to know that I am Brittany Bradford. I love the life I live and I try my hardest to live the life I love. I believe that a peaceful life is the best life

and life is whatever you make it. Purpose and
time. Just wait on it."

broken into two
a family
a person
she
her
them
they
life came
it hit hard
the family-
they scatter
different directions
different paths through life
good outcomes
some bad
each are
'stand alone, walk alone'
sometimes that just ain't right
she-
confused
something has captured her mind

'demons on her back like a life coach'

driving & stirring into all directions

light

dark

good vibes

bad ones

truth

lies

positivity

& destruction

her

that girl

she's seen it all

Frances ("Frankie") Croom

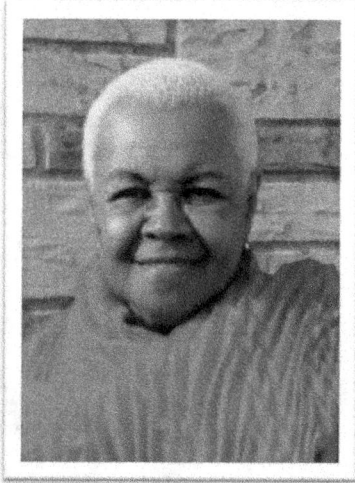

Greetings to my Blonde Sisters.

Hi, my name is Frankie and I have rocked my platinum blonde coif for the past 50 years. I've dabbled in color before, including being a red-head, but I always return to being a blonde because it is true......blondes have more fun! Both sexes admire my style and adventurous spirit, even during my travels in Europe. People have often mistaken my D.I.Y. (do-it-yourself) technique for high end salon talent.

My blondness releases my inner radiance and satiates my need to be noticed and stand out above all others. I feel like I'm walking the runway every day, all the time, and owning it!

I began my journey as a blonde back in the 1960's. Growing up, I was surrounded by women who celebrated their grey and silver hair. These women embraced their silver with such dignity, elegance and grace that I could not wait on Mother Nature. So, I did the next best thing. I took charge and went blonde at the age of 25. The initial brassy blonde look didn't give me what I wanted. After dabbling in varying degrees of blondness I finally discovered platinum blonde. I'm a purest. I don't do kits. I still do it the way I did back in the 60's. I buy 40 weight peroxide, B&W powder, and use Shimmer Lights shampoo to maintain the platinum effect.

My platinum hair is such a part of my signature style that friends and co-workers often don't recognize me when I allow my color to grow out. When people search for me they always look for my coif.

So if you are thinking about going blonde, stop thinking, and do it, even for a season of fun, you WILL have a good time.

Life is meant to be lived!

Love,

Frankie!!

The Feisty One

I met Frankie on March 19, 2013 at the iHop on Alabama Avenue SE in Washington, DC. We had a great dinner as we talked for approximately 1 hour. I learned a lot about Frankie during our conversation. She was the oldest of the ladies I interviewed, 74 years old.

Growing Up

Frankie lives in the same house she grew up in; her Grandmother's and Mother's house. Growing up in DC was fun. There was less crime. You could fight somebody and end up becoming the best of friends. You could stay in the park all night long and nobody would bother you.

Frankie liked going to Hains Point. Drill Team – Griffith Stadium[48] on the corner of 7th and Florida Avenue. That's where they did all their school military activities. It was fun living in DC. Frankie's best friend's Grandmother was a caretaker at the Frederick Douglas Home. Used to go up there to play. Her friend's

Grandmother would make them dust before they could go play. Growing up in DC was historical and interesting.

Frankie attended Birney Elementary School. She graduated from Dunbar High School in 1957. Paul Laurence Dunbar High School was originally named Preparatory High School for Colored Youth and later known as M Street High School. Founded as an educational mission at the Fifteenth Street Presbyterian Church, Dunbar was America's first public high school for black students. It was later the academic high school, with other schools related to vocational or technical training goals. It was known for its excellent academics, enough so that some black parents moved to Washington, DC specifically so their children could attend it. Its faculty was paid well by the standards of the time, earning parity pay to Washington's white school teachers because they were federal employees. It also boasted a remarkably high number of graduates who went on to higher education, and a generally successful student body.

Frankie attended Howard University for 2 years, and then dropped out to get married. Didn't pledge a sorority while she was at Howard because she wanted to go Delta. She was dating a football player and found out one of the Delta's was interested in him. Figured it was going to be a problem. Pledging back then was wild, and Frankie wasn't going to let anyone take advantage of her.

While attending Howard, Frankie had friends from Montclair, Trenton and Alabama. All her friends were physical ed majors. One year she didn't stay home for Christmas, but went to Pat's home in Trenton, NJ. Her family was AKA.[49] There was an upcoming AKA Ball. The family bought Frankie a gown so she could attend the ball. After that, Frankie went home with someone every Christmas. She learned to play Pinochle at Howard in the Student Room at

Douglas Hall. You had to get there early, 6am, to get your seat.

The Dancer

One of Frankie's dreams was to be a dancer. She was going to audition for the Ballet Academy of New York. Frankie and her girlfriend didn't know you had to be single to be part of the Ballet Academy, so they got married a week before the audition, which disqualified them. Frankie got an attitude. It only hurt her, but she was upset.

During the 70's and 80's Frankie was a Go-Go Dancer at the military clubs. It all got started when Frankie attended a party at Bolling Air Force Base.[50] She started dancing and cutting up. She was approached by another dancer who told her she was a good dancer. The dancer suggested that Frankie join them. Frankie said, "Join you doing what!" The lady told Frankie to come to one of her workshops. She did, and joined the group of Go-Go dancers. "Never knew there were so many military clubs in her life." Frankie was a Go-Go dancer for 5 years, and got great tips.

Just Stuff

Frankie had 4 children. Youngest boy was killed when he was 18. She spoiled her children, but they are good kids. Two in DC, youngest in Leesburg.

Frankie still likes to party, bad hip and all. Can't let the deteriorating hip get in the way. Every Monday, Wednesday and Friday Frankie walks 3 miles and goes to the pool.

She's been dating a guy for 30 years. Not getting married. Her mother told her, "if it's not broke, don't fix it."

If Frankie can get up every morning, dress herself, do the things she wants to do, and go to church on Sunday, she's happy. She celebrated her 75th birthday in North Carolina, with a surprise trip to Cape Hatteras with her family and friends. They rented a 7 bedroom house for a week. This was the best birthday party Frankie ever had, and she will never forget it.

"As you get older you realize, even if you argue with someone, say what you want to say and just let things go. Hug and kiss and keep it moving. Life is too short. Don't hold any grudges. When you hold grudges, they wear and tear on you, causing high blood pressure. What's gonna happen will happen."

When Frankie goes on vacation, she turns her cell phone off. Tells her children not to call her when she's on vacation. There's nothing she can do. She's out of town. If someone dies or gets sick, let her know about it when she gets back in the city. Don't call her and mess up her vacation, because she's not going to cut it short. "Realistically, if I'm over in Europe, I'm not going to cut my vacation short."

World Traveler

Frankie takes a cruise twice a year. In 2008 she went to Italy, France and Spain. Flew over and picked up the Voyage of the Sea. This year she's going to Hawaii, via the Norwegian, Grand Turks and the Dominican Republic, back to Amsterdam, Belgium, Paris and London in August 2014, and to China in October 2015.

Frankie is very adventurous. She's ridden a camel in Cairo. The tour guide didn't tell her she needed to lean back while getting on the camel. Told her when you go up the hill you lean forward, and vice versa when you go down a hill. Frankie rode the camel to the Pyramids, which took 45 minutes to 1 hour. She has ridden an elephant at Soul Circus. She travelled to Ireland with her parents when she was younger. Frankie has a dream of going on a safari, but said couldn't live in the desert. "Too much Sand, Sand, Sand."

Work Life

Frankie worked at the Department of Commerce as a Benefits Specialist, handling Health Events, Retirement, and Insurance and Compensation. Did this for 31 years.[51] She went into the government right after high school.

Frankie worked as a pre-school teacher for the Department of Recreation for 3-4 year olds for 2 years. She was one of the first teachers-aides. Worked in the Navy Department and went on to work at St. Elizabeth's.

She currently works at the Verizon Center.[52] She started out as a Hostess in 1997, and is now a Marshall. Frankie can work most of the positions at Verizon Center. She helps people to their seats, and handles relocations. For Wizards and Caps games she works downstairs with 3 employees under her. They feed the staff. When she goes into the bowl, her family can find her by her hair, even if she has on a hat. Just look for long nails and blonde hair.

Working at Verizon Center is fun, not like a job. Once they start stressing her out, she'll quit.

The Red Hat Lady

Frankie always wanted to join the Red Hat Society,[53] so she formed her own chapter. The Red Hat Society's primary purpose is social interaction and bonding among women. A founder or leader of a local chapter of the Red Hat Society is usually referred to as a "Queen." Members 50 and over are called "Red Hatters" and wear red hats and purple attire to all functions. A woman under age 50 may also become a member, but she wears a pink hat and lavender attire to the Society's events until reaching her 50th birthday. She is referred to as a "Pink Hatter." During her birthday month (or the Society's birthday month of April), a member might wear her colors in reverse, i.e., a purple or lavender hat and red or pink attire.

There are two ways of belonging to the Red Hat Society: as a Queen (usually leader of a local chapter; however, no Queen is required to lead a chapter) and as a Supporting Member. Membership dues are paid annually, respective to the attendee's role, to the Red Hat Society. Interested prospects can register to become members online.

So, once while Frankie was in Tyson's Corner, she went to a Tea Party. Red Hatters were at another table and caught her attention. The rest is history; she formed the Hatastic Divas. The Hatastic Divas get together once a month, every third Saturday. They drink wine and eat cheese.

Other activities have included going to the Wax Museum, shopping, spending several days in Ocean City every September, and having a yearly Christmas party. Frankie wears red hats, cowboy hats, and baseball caps. Her baseball cap says Queen. On your birthday you wear a purple hat and red dress. The red hatter dues are $35 for the Queen and $20 for members.

When the ladies go to Ocean City they stay in a condo right off the boardwalk. The Hatastic Divas consist of 6 members. They have their meeting and then they party. Four head to the beach on the Thursday of Sunfest[54] week and the two remaining members come later. Four tents of vendors and food. Chinet plates, no time to wash dishes.

My time with Frankie was priceless. Thank goodness I found her. She initially told me to meet her at Denny's on Alabama Avenue SE. I've driven on Alabama Avenue many times, but for the life of me I never remembered seeing a Denny's restaurant. After driving past the iHop on Alabama Avenue about 5 times I parked my car, walked into iHop, and who did I find? Frankie. Her energy and enthusiasm lit up the restaurant. Quality time shared with another sister.

J. Hammond

Yes, that's my real name, lol. I'm a 21 year old, adventurous black woman! I love my vibrant, gorgeous blonde hair. My hair is natural, and I have thick blonde beautiful LOCKS!!!!! I love being and having natural hair. Being blonde was a decision that I made about two years ago before I got my locks. I've tried every color under the sun. From crazy HOTT PINK, PURPLE, and BLUE to JET BLACK, BROWN and finally BLONDE!!!!!!

My inspiration is the thought of myself always being ORIGINAL! I've always wanted to stand out and be my own person. A lot of women may be blonde, but not my shade of blonde. My shade comes from within, if that makes any sense. I always try to be a ball of sunshine to others. We are all UNIQUE in our own way!!!!

My biggest passion is doing natural hair and make-up as well. I get excited anytime I get a new client and have the opportunity to make them look beautiful and satisfied at the same time. To me, that is satisfaction enough. I have a goal of becoming a master at my craft and starting my own business with a natural hair care salon. I believe that not only black women, but ALL women should embrace themselves, and love themselves, and find their originality to perfectly fit their swag!!!!!

Making Women Look Beautiful

I met J. and her dog Star on Feb. 16, 2013. Star is an American Pitbull, 5 months old, and adorable.

J.'s parents couldn't decide on a name for her. Her sisters are named Max and Unique. J. was the last baby, so her parents gave her a letter and said "we'll call it a day."

During our conversation J. said "A shade of blonde comes from within." If you recall from the Introduction, Dr. Tony Fallone stated "hair color is the root of a person's personality." He also stated "being blonde is not a hair color, but a state of mind." J. sees blondes all the time, but people comment that they have never seen her shade of blonde. She feels people put out a certain light. She has often heard people say " She's glowing." She tries to stay as positive as possible.

Her Passions

Doing hair and makeup are J.'s passions. She gets excited when she gets a new client. J. makes sure the client gets exactly what they want, and that they are really satisfied. The last booking was a bridal shower. They wanted a natural look. J. is all about helping women look beautiful.

J. is starting a foundation with her Mom for women who have problems in their household, teenagers coming into themselves, just feeling comfortable with themselves, being beautiful and knowing they don't need to change. If she can be a part of that, knowing she helped them along, then she's good with that.

The foundation is in the beginning stages. J.'s Mom is also starting a country club across the street from their home. Getting all the paperwork in order. Looking for investors. Country club, restaurant. Mom is a paralegal and started her own business. Helps people with court cases. She's doing pretty well. Her second business.

J. wants to master her craft and start her own natural hair care salon. She's so busy. Tried to start school, but needed funds to go to school. Was told she didn't qualify for financial aid. Either had to get pregnant, join the military or have a baby. She was like "Ok." I found this rather disturbing. Why do you have to get pregnant and have a baby if you want to further your education. Anyway, J. is working to save for school. Works 2 jobs. She's busy, busy, busy. She wants to go to cosmetology school. There's a woman that has a natural hair class, starts every second Monday of the month. J. is going to do this class to gain accreditation.

J. is very talented and likes to make her own hair products. She colors them. Makes her stuff just for her. Natural shea butter oil, lemon oil, actual lemon and some other stuff. Lemon enhances the blonde. Bed head shampoo, curly hair, enhances the curls. Smells really good.

The Story, The Movement

Growing up wasn't easy. J. had to fend for herself because her parents weren't there for her a lot. Now that she's getting older she appreciates things a lot more. When J. saw the Black Girls Gone Blonde website she thought it was a really good idea, empowering black women. All about bringing women together, helping them find themselves, even young women. Going through things, offer to get them help. J. would just like to get the message out that there is help and support available for women that need it. Just be an inspiration to other people.

During our interview I talked about Brittany working with the special needs children. We talked about the challenges people may be going through, and how some of the issues described in the book might help make a difference.

She Loves Kids

I asked J. "What touches your heart?" She told me the thing she loves most, 6 nieces and nephews and 10 great nieces and nephews. Anytime she can get everyone together with the kids, she's in heaven. She loves working with the kids.

Just J.

J. works at the Library of Congress. She does hair in her home, or she will come to you. She wanted locks since she was 9 years old, and will transition to SisterLocks[55]eventually. Her eyebrows were beautiful and perfect. She did them. Pencil and brush. Her tongue and eyebrow are pierced.

J. was the quietest of the ladies I interviewed, but you know what they say about the quiet ones. WATCH OUT!!!

Candice Johnson

My name is Candice and I am Blonde, Black and Beautiful. I chose blonde because I wanted something new, different, and something that best suited me and my personality; "FUN, FREE, AND FIERCE, with two snaps. Besides, I hold a license in cosmetology and get bored with one look. I'm always looking for ways to reinvent myself.   I am not my hair and should be recognized as the multi-talented individual that I am. I will continue to challenge all obstacles with full determination. I refuse to be defeated and will "Win" in the end. I will continue to stand out, express my own individuality and creativity and will not conform to what is expected. My mentor Daisaku Ikeda[56] says, "To lead a life in which we are inspired and can inspire others, our hearts have to be alive; they have to be filled with passion and enthusiasm. To achieve that, we need the courage to "live true to ourselves."

The Super Star

I had the pleasure of meeting Candice on March 2, 2013. My first thought when she opened her door was "OMG, she's breathtaking." I started our interview by telling Candice why I was blonde and how I felt a connection, a bond with other black women that were also blonde. I told her I was driving to work one morning and the thought popped into my head to do something called "Black Girls Gone Blonde." I also expressed my surprise that someone else hadn't already written a book similar to this one. We came to the conclusion that God wanted me to do this. Before the interview actually started I told Candice my blue Timex watch story. She got a big kick out of it.

Growing Up

Candice was born in Washington, DC and raised in the house where we conducted the interview. She later moved to Riverdale, Maryland when her Mother remarried. The house was left to her when her grandfather passed away. She has two siblings; Tonika and Damien. They are all 5 years apart, and each has a different father. Candice is the oldest. She and her siblings grew up in a dysfunctional household where she was physically and verbally abused by her mom, and molested by her stepfather. Candice relied heavily on her friends (Chiquita Cee-Cee, Nicole, Gashiya, Jamilla, Emesha and Tara), since their homes represented a safe haven when her Mom would often put her out of the house. Her Mom was 32 years old when she married a man that was 19. He was addicted to crack, and physically abused Candice's Mother. Candice had to grow up fast, having the responsibility of raising her brother and sister. She and her siblings went through tough times in the household, but Candice told them, "It's all in the choices you make and you can't use your environment or upbringing as an excuse to not want better for yourself."

Candice chose to go a different route, she went to the right; her siblings chose to go left. Her siblings were constantly in and out of trouble in school and with the law. Candice's biological Father wasn't active in her life due to his battle with mental illness and drug abuse. She was determined that she was not going to be like her Mother or Father. She wanted something better for herself.

Candice told herself the next time her Mom put her out, she was never coming back. Well, that next time came. With nowhere to go, Candice then moved in with the Gibbs family, where they took on the role of being parents to her. Candice was 16. She obtained her first job at Springhill Lake Recreation Center with her Dad, Austin Gibbs. She worked very hard to provide for herself by working three jobs at a time and also with the help of her grandparents Miles Jones and Judith Catlin. She was determined not to have to return home with her mother and stepfather. Candice later went on to work at a law firm with her friend Jamilla. She went from the mailroom to taking a course with Piper Marbury Rudnick and Wolfe where she obtained her paralegal certificate. After receiving her certificate she was offered a job at Latham & Watkins as a Legal Secretary, and by this time was able to afford her very first apartment. Candice persevered because she is the strongest of the 3 children. There is always at least one strong one in the bunch, and she needed to be strong for Damien and Tonika. She was their mother figure where her Mom would sometimes lack. Today she still acts as a mother figure to her siblings.

Hair Dynamics

Candice has been blonde for the last 4 to 5 years. She changed her hair color to blonde because she needed a change. Candice was going through a breakup, and it seems that whenever women breakup, we either need to change our hair, get a mani/pedi, or spend money. She shaved her head and wore her hair dark for a few days. The dark hair was too dull and boring. Candice needed something to give her hair that pop. So here's what she did. She went to the beauty supply store, purchased some BW2 and some 40 volume peroxide.

Candice said "that's what you have to use to get it really light; otherwise you would have to lighten your hair in stages." She liked the new platinum look and was getting compliments. She was probed with questions like, "What color is that? How did you do it?" Candice was rockin' it, and has been blonde ever since.

Prior to going blonde, Candice's hair was dark brown. When she went on a casting call she was either wearing wigs or weaves. During this time Candice's hair was almost shoulder length, and it was just kinda boring. DC is so conservative. Everyone looks the same, and Candice does not like to look like everyone else. Candice feels that there is always a specific type...you have to have shoulder length hair and feathered blowouts or what they consider to be ethnically ambiguous when you go on castings. There is also beauty in short hair. You may get a lot of "no's" before you get that "yes." Candice isn't going to let the "no's" stop her from pursuing her dream, and from making a difference and break barriers for other black women.

"It's rough, but I will continue to challenge all obstacles with full determination." ~Candice Johnson

The Model

Candice started modeling when she was a teenager, and she always had a fear of succeeding. She sometimes still hears her mother's words, "You ain't shit and you will never be shit, and no one will want you." This discouraged Candice, and delayed the pursuit of her goals, dreams and ambitions. She eventually realized that those words from her mother were false. Candice was determined to prove her mother wrong, but her modeling career took second stage at this point in her life. Now she's 39, and modeling is center stage again.

As an African-American woman in the modeling business, Candice faces many challenges. Candice's current challenge is the scrutiny she encounters in this modeling industry, ranging from her being slightly curvy, African-American, not tall enough, and most of all, categorized as an " Urban Model" because she has short blonde, natural hair. She has a universal look and believes she can also be considered high fashion. Unfortunately, when she goes on castings and go sees, they immediately want to put her in urban apparel. They oftentimes also say Candice is too commercial. She has even noticed at certain fashion shows she has done, it was like she was never even there or took part. Looking at photos from the events, there were only a few of her and tons of the other models who were not African-American. One of the designers, who was African-American, did not choose Candice to wear her garments. The models chosen were all Caucasian.

Candice's question is "How is it that other ethnicities can alter their hair color and be considered high fashion, but because I chose to alter my natural hair color and become a blonde, I'm urban? To me, there is no difference. "

Candice intends to stay blonde unless she gets a gig that requires her to change, but she wants to stay true to herself. However, she also knows that sometimes this may be required of her. It's part of the business. She believes it's time for barriers to be broken.

In the 2013 March edition of Numero, a prominent international fashion magazine, white, 16-year-old model, Ondria Hardin, poses in full-on, full-bodied bronzed hue. The editorial spread was called, of all things, "African Queen." [57]

Ondria is signed to Ford Models, along with numerous other women, from varying races and nationalities. I went to the Ford Models website and saw 4 beautiful black women signed to the agency that could have gotten this gig. Why not use Kelly, Samira, CiCi or Damaris Lewis for the African Queen shoot? Candice had also visited the Ford website and saw 3 black models on the first page. This was very disheartening and disturbing to Candice. She questions why others of different ethnicities can change their hair color to blonde and still be considered high fashion, but when black women change their hair color to blonde they're considered urban. Is this discrimination? Did racism really end or is it still here but in different forms?

There's more to life than being a music video vixen or modeling street apparel consisting of jeans, sweatshirts and sneakers, but that's what Candice often encounters. Blonde, natural hair can be high fashion too. Candice's view is "why not bring in something new instead of always casting dark-skinned women? There are different shades of what we call black. We are all beautiful and different in our own way."

On a recent trip to New York, Candice stopped by a casting that happens every Wednesday. She didn't have her portfolio, but decided since she was in New York she would drop in. The desk attendant asked if she had her portfolio. She told him she didn't have it.

He probed her with more questions, one being how tall are you? Candice is 5'9" and the guy told her "we like our girls to be a smidget taller than you – we want our girls to be 5'10." The way he looked Candice up and down made her feel some kind of way - strange. His next question was "have you tried any commercial agencies, cause we're into high fashion? Candice's thought was "so you ask that to say what?" She was humble about the situation. She smiled, said thank you and have a good day, and left. Candice feels she is often turned down because she is African-American, and because of her hair color. Casting agencies want Asians, red heads, tall Caucasians with long blonde hair and brunettes or ethnically ambiguous.

Candice understands that it's all in what the client wants, but believes there is market for people that look like her. "I can appreciate beauty of all types, but I can better relate to someone that looks like me. It's a rough market."

The Entrepreneur

In addition to modeling, Candice is an entrepreneur. She is a trained cosmetologist – been doing hair for 20+ years, and also does makeup. She graduated from Robert's Hair Institute in 1996. She didn't immediately start doing hair after graduation, but discovered this was her niche and decided to return to the beauty industry full time, where she helps others express their own individuality through hair. We all know the saying, "when you look good, you feel good." Well, it makes Candice happy when she makes someone else feel happy about their appearance. She's passionate about what she does. Candice had a business in Largo, but the rent was killing her. She wasn't making a profit, so she decided to work from home. Candice has managed several Hair Cuttery's and Great Clips, in addition to also being a part-time Instructor at Harmon Beauty School. She has also taught braiding courses at PG Community College. This woman is a jack of all trades.

Candice Now

Modeling is center stage. Candice says, "To accomplish all that she has in the modeling industry at the age of 38 is amazing. She wants to tell the world and everyone out there to live out loud and live your dream, it is never too late, and age is nothing but a number." People ask Candice often if she is too old to be modeling, and she respectfully says, "No, I'm not."

In 2011 Candice submitted her pictures to Wilhelmina Philadelphia[58] and she was signed. During 2012 Candice decided not to renew her contract. She decided Wilhelmina Philadelphia wasn't the agency for her. Candice declined to go into detail regarding her experience with Wilhelmina Philadelphia, but she was there for a year and was never booked for a gig and/or sent on go sees. She networked and found her own gigs; determination got her to where she is now. She's by herself and for herself – so she might as well be a freelance model.

Candice has done NY and Philly Fashion Week, and Soul Afrik Fashion Week, which is endorsed by Russell Simons, two magazine publications Swerv Magazine and Natural Care Magazine. She has also participated in various charity runway events. One charity event in particular is Angels for Animals at the Stotesbury Mansion in Philadelphia. It was amazing. She had the best time ever.

The Actress

On March 29, 2013, I saw the encore performance of Bound and Gagged; Bound by Fear, Gagged by Love, which focuses on domestic violence against women. Candice played the role of Patience, a woman in an abusive relationship. She gets my Super Star vote. This was a very uplifting experience for Candice as she too experienced domestic violence... so it hit very close to home.

Bound and Gagged was written, directed and produced by Shannon Whren. Some of the story is based on true events experienced by Ms.

Whren. All proceeds from the play went to Devine Networks, to help abused women get out of their abusive situation.

I've also learned that Candice has appeared on House of Cards[59], episodes 5, 12 and 13, and was recently called back for Season Two.

She has found love and is very happy with her partner Nicola Jones. Life couldn't be better.

Last, but not least, Candice is working on several projects with her modeling and acting career. She recently had a spread in Desirable Magazine LLC. This would make her third publication. Always working on being the best she can be. I know Candice is destined to be a star. Let me rephrase that, Candice is a star!!

"Follow your dreams, it's never too late, age is nothing but a number." ~Candice Johnson

Antoinette Barnes

Antoinette wanted to try something new. Blondes have more fun, right? My hair has been purple, fuchsia, orange you name it, I tried it. I even wore a blonde streaked Jheri Curl. In 2000 I decided to go blonde. Women were dying their hair blonde during this time, but it wasn't really big. I color my own hair, using Neutral Kalediocolors with Clairol 40 lift. The lighter I bleach my hair the brighter my spirit. Kudos to my barber, "Ron", owner of Ron Cut Masters located in Waldorf, MD who keeps me looking good.

The Dancer

I had the pleasure of meeting Antoinette Barnes on Feb. 16, 2013. Her energy was amazing... such positivity. Antoinette was 53 when we met.

About Toni

Antoinette Maria Barnes aka "Toni" described herself as creative, enthusiastic and dependable. She was raised in the DC Metropolitan area and currently lives in Waldorf, MD. Antoinette has a Bachelor's Degree in Business Mgmt. & Administration, and has 27 years of Federal Government service under her belt. She currently works for the Department of Homeland Security.

Antoinette is the proud mother of Tiana (30) and Anthony (24) who recently received their Masters and Bachelor's degrees, respectively. She has one brother . . . Andre, and assures everyone "her Mom, Paulette, only has "one" daughter.

Antoinette's passion is dance, and she received the vast amount of her dance instruction with "Bren-Car Dancers" in Washington, DC. Her love for dance and fitness have presented opportunities to choreograph ballet, jazz, and liturgical pieces for Saint Teresa Avila Catholic Church Dance Ministry and various other churches in the DC area for over 15 years. She is now embarking on her own venture as the founding Director of Women of Worship (WOW) Liturgical Dance Ministry. Antoinette continues her dance and exercise regime to this day by attending dance workshops as well as Zumba and kick-boxing classes.

Antoinette loves the fact that she has been given the opportunity to evangelize through dance. Working with the youth at her church is inspirational as well as a way to keep her grounded. "The respect and love shared for one another and the relationships that have formed watching the children grow up can't be described in words." The children come to dance as young as age 5 and some are now in their 30's. Antoinette loves all of them as if they were her own. She never imagined herself as a role model and sometimes still has to pinch herself because she knows the kids believe in her when she doesn't. Antoinette commented, "I cherish the gifts the creator has given me and humbly give back with an open heart."

Life Obstacle

Antoinette had to learn to love herself ... One month before her wedding day her fiancé walked away. Antoinette attempted to end her life at age 25. It took her more than 10 years to climb out of that funk, rebuild her self-esteem and learn to love herself again. Antoinette told me "life is full of setbacks and sometimes it takes a long time to recover. The important thing is to pick yourself up, brush yourself off and keep moving on...take chances...and most of all, Live! You only get to do it once."

Brandi Nichole Dickerson

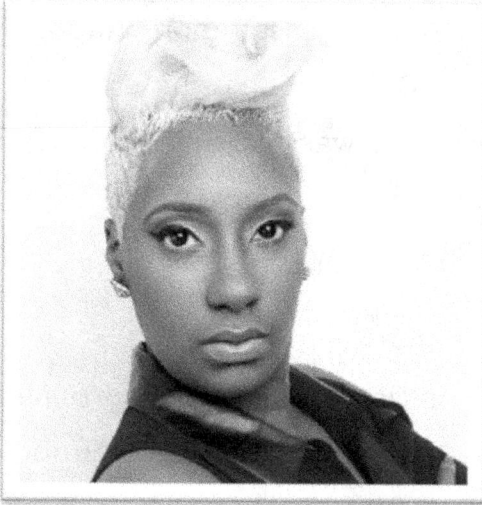

Brandi has been blonde since March 2013. She decided to go blonde because she is a hair stylist and she wanted to take her career up a notch by becoming a celebrity stylist. In order to do that, she needed to do something that would make her stand out, something that would make people look at her and say "Yes", she is a celebrity stylist. More so, it was to put her in the celebrity element and move her forward as a hair stylist.

She Came Back

I met Brandi at 11:00am on August 12, 2013 at Panera Bread on Baltimore National Pike in Baltimore, MD. It was sunny and cool outside. My ride from DC was relaxing. The closer I got to my destination, the more excited I got thinking about my meeting with Brandi.

About Brandi

Brandi is from Eastern Shore Maryland - Salisbury, MD. The majority of Brandi's family is still in Salisbury, however she has one brother that also lives in Baltimore. Brandi moved to Baltimore for career advancement. She's been a hair stylist for 12 years. When she first got her license, she started at a salon in Salisbury, MD but things weren't moving forward because it was predominantly a booth rental salon. She decided to go to work at a Smart Style in Walmart. While working in Smart Style, some of the customers mentioned that Brandi didn't do hair like she was from there. Brandi created a whole different style, so she decided to move where it was bigger than her hometown, which was Baltimore, MD. When she decided to move to Baltimore she worked at 2 other salons, became an educator at a beauty school, and then decided to leave the beauty school and open her first salon, Studio 77.

The Celebrity Stylist

Brandi goes by Brandi Nichole in the hair industry and specializes in short hair. She used to wear her hair long, but decided to cut it short to try something different. She believes short hair opens up a woman's beauty, enables you to see her facial features, enhances, and also gives a younger look to women. Brandi loves the reaction she gets from women when they decide to go with a short hair style. While she loves doing short hair, she also does natural blowouts, specializes in healthy hair, runway hair and onset hair and makeup. She also does a lot of cut and color, some weaves, but predominantly short and natural hair. Moving forward in her career, Brandi now owns Bee CHIC Imagez LLC.[60] She started the freelance business in June

2012, and then moved to a physical site in October 2012. She made some changes to grow the business, so she decided to relocate her business to a home office and turn it into an styling agency.

The reason Brandi came up with Bee CHIC Imagez was because CHIC is an acronym that stands for Confidence, Healing, Independence and Courage. Bee is Brandi's nickname, and she also believes your hair is a part of your full image. So when Bee CHIC Imagez came about, it was just basically a reflection of what she has been through and where she wants women to go and be. She wants women to be confident, to be healed, to be independent, and to be courageous through their image. Being the woman that they were designed to be.

Brandi wants women to know that the sky is the limit. "We don't have to limit ourselves to our current situation. We don't have to allow life circumstances we go through to hinder or keep us from our dreams."

The Accident

Three years ago, when Brandi was married, she was getting out of the shower and she slipped on the floor of her stand-up shower. While trying to catch her balance, she went through the glass shower door. Not plexiglass, but 100% real glass. Brandi literally cut her arm down to the bone.

Brandi's husband at the time, was home and on his way out the front door for work. He heard Brandi scream and ran in the back room to see what happened. He rushed her to the hospital.

At the time of the accident Brandi didn't have any insurance, but was rushed to the hospital anyway. They were able to stitch her arm up until she could see a hand doctor. This happened on a Thursday evening. By the following Tuesday morning Brandi was going into surgery. The incident happened the week before Thanksgiving, so the week of Thanksgiving Brandi was in a cast.

Brandi was mistreated because she didn't have any insurance. After surgery, she had to wait four weeks before she started physical therapy. Technically, Brandi should have started therapy a week after surgery. So it was harder for her to heal properly, because scar tissue had developed. She went to therapy and had lost all feeling in her hand, which resulted in Brandi being out of work for nine months. She couldn't do hair, and had to close her salon. Thank God, she was able to collect unemployment from when she was teaching at the school. As time went on, Brandi got depressed because she couldn't do hair; she couldn't do what she loves.

Brandi reached a point of depression and treated her hand like it didn't belong to her. At first she gave up. Wasn't using her hand, wasn't moving it. In her mind she thought it was the end. Thought she would never be able to do hair again. She enrolled in college to try and get a degree because she thought she wouldn't be able to use her hand. So instead of putting her hand to use, she disowned her right hand and started trying to build up the strength in the left hand. That's when she decided she didn't want to give up on her dream.

Her hand is a blessing. She could have waddled in her depression and decided she couldn't use her hand, but when you're passionate about something, it's like you're passion is reignited. It helps you to move forward and get to your success.

One day she decided she couldn't go to therapy anymore because she lost her insurance. So what did she do? She created her own therapy by getting back in the salon and doing what she loves most. She was learning to do hair all over again. She had to learn how to properly hold the comb and scissors, learn to hold the curling iron, learn to do weave again. She was determined that she wasn't going to let her situation handicap her, and keep her from being a successful celebrity hair stylist.

Currently, she doesn't have any feeling in her hand, but she still uses her craft as a form of therapy. When she left the regular therapist she had regained half of her strength. Had to learn to type and use the computer. From there, her therapy was doing what she loved most, doing hair.

Weather changes cause her to experience pain. Fingers are numb and restricted. It's been three years since the accident. She cut nerves and tendons. The surgeons told her it would take time before she got any feeling back in her hand. Every now and again she feels pain, and the doctors told her that's an indication that she's healing.

Brandi was wearing a beautiful gold bracelet on her right wrist during our interview. I noticed a scar just below the bracelet, so I asked if that was the scar from the accident. That was the scar. It was originally a 1 inch scar, but the doctors cut her any kind of way, resulting in a longer scar.

Miraculously, the hospital paid Brandi's hospital bill. It was a $12,000 surgery. When the hospital saw that Brandi didn't have any insurance, she applied for assistance, filled out paperwork. Brandi submitted info that they requested. A month after the surgery she started receiving bills in the mail. Subsequently she started receiving letters telling her that her bills were paid because she qualified for assistance. What a blessing!!

Brandi experiences pain when she does too many heads, turns her hand wrong, or with cold weather. Cold weather is really bad, and she has to wear a heated glove. Rainy weather is the worst. Took her six months to get back to where she was before the accident.

Her passion for doing hair brought her out of her depression. She can't do anything else. Tried other things; worked in the medical field, medical billing. She was often turned away because she only had hair experience and beauty education. She honestly couldn't see herself doing anything else. What she decided to do, unlike most hair stylist who do hair, but also do something else on the side, like daycare or something in the medical field, she learned her industry and decided to tap into those areas where she could make more money than just being behind the chair. That's what led Brandi to her specialty as a celebrity stylist. She aspires to work with Kerry Washington, Halle Berry, K Michelle, Chrisette Michelle-she's Brandi's #1, Tamala Mann. There's a long list of people she would like to work with, and her plan is to use her upcoming talk show to publicize her hair business. Brandi will also attend networking events with high profile potential clients. She's walking by faith and reaching out to their assistants and publicists email addresses, making herself known.

A Perfect Day

I wanted to know what a perfect day looked like for Brandi, and she told me, "A perfect day consists of going to her salon, doing 6 or 7 clients, but in between promoting herself, getting unexpected calls resulting from weeks prior when she's sewn seeds reaching out to people. Wrapping up her work day, going home and basically about being productive and feeling a sense of accomplishment from the things she set out to do on her slow days. Making phone calls, sending out emails, connecting with people." So, Brandi's perfect day would be just reaping the benefits of pushing and making the right connections and being productive.

The Oprah Effect

As we concluded the interview we started to talk about a show I had seen on CNBC. The show was called "The Oprah Effect" and it showed various business owners, authors, etc. and the impact Oprah's recognition of their products on her show had on their business success. I mentioned how wonderful it would be if we could get our book in front of Oprah, Queen Latifah, and Ellen Degeneres, and the impact it would have on our lives and the lives of millions of women. We discussed how important it is for this book to make a difference, be uplifting, give hope, and inspire.

Conclusion

As I read and edited everyone's story I became touched by how personal the conversations were. When I met with each of the ladies, I felt a certain closeness. A closeness like I had known the ladies for years.

They were an inspiring group of ladies, and I'm grateful and honored that I had the pleasure of sharing quality time with them. They're my sisters for life.

I think the general consensus of everyone I talked to was don't let past experiences stand in your way, keep it moving, it's never too late to go after your dreams, be strong, stay determined, and leave the past behind.

I was trying to think of a song that would symbolize the message I was trying to convey by writing this book. I love a song I initially heard many years ago performed by Sweetback called *You Will Rise.*

You Will Rise (Composed by Stuart Cottonbelly Matthewman - 1997 Epic/Sony - Performed by Sweetback)

I got a story that must be heard,
About a little girl who wished she was a bird,
She was unhappy livin' in her ghetto cage,
But it gave her hope when her sweet grandma would say:
(Baby, you will rise)
Rise
(Limit is the skies)
The skies
(Don't let nobody fill your head with their lies)
Nobody.. fill your head with lies
(Baby, you will rise)
Rise
(Never compromise)
Compromise
(Milk and honey is waitin' for you on the other side)
Waitin' for you on the other side
Yeah

She had a burning desire to go far,

And she had lively hopes of reaching every star

One day she'd leave this place,

But never forget her people's face

And when she found her dreams,

She'd come back and proclaim:

   (Baby, you will rise)

Rise

(Limit is the skies)

The skies

(Don't let nobody fill your head with their lies)

Nobody.. fill your head with lies

(Baby, you will rise)

Rise

(Never compromise)

Compromise

(Milk and honey is waitin' for you on the other

side)

Waitin' for you on the other side

You will rise..

(Baby, you will rise)

Rise

(Limit is the skies)

The skies

(Don't let nobody fill your head with their lies)

Nobody.. fill your head with lies

(Baby, you will rise)

Rise

(Never compromise)

Compromise

(Milk and honey is waitin' for you on the other

side)

Waitin' for you on the other side

Got a burning in my heart,

To keep it real and do my part

Got a burning in my soul,

To recognize where I'm from, yeah

Got a burning in my heart,

To keep it real and do my part

Got a burning in my soul

To recognize where I'm from, yeah

The Author

Joani is an Adjunct Professor with subject matter expertise in Finance. She launched a consulting and internet marketing business, Nothing In Between, LLC in March 2011. The mission for the consulting prong of the business is to motivate and assist aspiring entrepreneurs create the business of their dreams. The internet marketing prong of the business focuses on one of Joani's passions - affiliate and internet marketing.

Joani loves travelling, playing tennis, reading, bikram yoga, working out, and classical music, especially classical guitar. She studied classical guitar with Scott Matejicka at the Peabody Conservatory, and practiced with a chamber music group during her studies. She also loves dogs, and has a very special place in her heart for West Highland Terriers (Westies). Fluffy, her Westie, and best friend for 13 years, was put to rest on May 14, 2012.

Other books by Joani Ward

(available at **www.joaniwardbooks.com**)
include:

You Don't Have To Be Broke: So Wake Up,
Shake It Up, And Make A Change

Business Quotations Every Entrepreneur Should
Know: 52 Weeks of Motivation And Inspiration

Create Your WordPress Website in 27 Minutes:
Believe Me It's Possible

How To Write And Self Publish Your Own Book:
7 Steps to a Finished Product in 30 Days

Other Contacts

William Maxwell – WM Graphics

Email: Maxwell@wmgraphics.com

Website: www.wmprintshop.com

Maya Indigo – Maya Indigo Photography

mayaindigophotography@gmail.com

www.mayaindigo.squarespace.com

Brandi Nichole Dickerson – Bee CHIC Imagez

www.beechicimagez.com

Candice Johnson – Off The Wall Hair & Style by CJ

www.vagaro.com/offthewallhairandstyle

Santa Leah Jones – 909 Design

http://www.houzz.com/professionals/s/909-Design

References

[a] Ilyin, Natalia. 2000. *Blonde Like Me: The Roots of the Blonde Myth in Our Culture.* New York, NY: Simon & Schuster.

[b] Pawlowski, A. "Firm Plans Resort Staffed by Blondes Only." CNN Travel. October 11, 2010. Accessed: May 12, 2012.

[c] Phillips, Kathy. 1999. *Vogue Book of Blondes.* New York, NY: Viking Studio.

[d] Pitman, Joanna. 2003. *On Blondes.* New York, NY: Bloomsbury.

[e] Roberts-Grey, Gina. "Brunettes Have More Beaus? Hair Color Facts." MSNBC.com. April 23, 2010. Accessed: May 12, 2012.

Wikipedia, The Free Encyclopedia

McKee, Shawn, "Do Blondes Have More Fun", eDiets, http://healthnews.ediets.com/lifestyle/do-blondes-have-more-fun.html Accessed March 30, 2013

Greene, D. Wendy. 2011. Black Women Can't Have Blonde Hair in the Workplace.
http://papers.ssrn.com/sol3/papers.cfm?abstract_id=1859662

Endnotes

---

[1] Clairol is in an industry which manufactures consumer products used in personal hygiene and beautification.

[2] Shirley Polykoff was an advertising genius employed by the Foote, Cone and Belding advertising agency.

[3] http://healthnews.ediets.com/lifestyle/do-blondes-have-more-fun.html

[4] http://en.wikipedia.org/wiki/Clairol#cite_note-1

[5] http://facts.randomhistory.com/blonde-hair-facts.html

[6]http://www.thefreelibrary.com/SAY+IT+LOUD.+I'M+BLOND+AND+I'M+PROUD%3B+Caroline+Storah+(all+natural,...-a080229289

[7]http://www.advertisinghall.org

[8] http://adage.com/article/special-report-the-advertising-century/ad-age-advertising-century-top-10-slogans/140156/

[9] http://en.wikipedia.org/wiki/Shirley_Polykoff

[10] A bean counter is a person, such as an accountant or financial officer, who is concerned with quantification, especially to the exclusion of other matters.

[11] http://www.hairboutique.com/tips/tip8018.htm

[12] http://www.youtube.com/user/herbalessences?v=AI5UIP-qTs8

[13] http://www.youtube.com/watch?v=89_CtYEE2k4

[14] http://en.wikipedia.org/wiki/Clairol

[15] http://facts.randomhistory.com/blonde-hair-facts.html

[16] http://www.ask.com/question/who-discovered-hydrogen-peroxide

[17] http://www.theatlantic.com/health/archive/2013/02/the-

original-blonde-bombshell-used-actual-bleach-on-her-head/273333/

[18] BW2 is an extra-strength, dedusted lightener that provides colorists the ultimate creative control over the lightening process.

[19] A clear liquid developer that provides a translucent liquid gel consistency for predictable hair color and lightening results every time. Ideal for bottle application, it is designed for use with permanent color and all powder and liquid lighteners.

[20] The lightening of the hair.

[21] Blonde women are often referred to as "Dumb Blondes." The "Dumb Blonde" joke may be rooted in the 1775 satirical play Les curiosites de la Foire, in which a high-class blonde, French prostitute named Rosalie Duthe is portrayed as being less than intelligent.

[22] http://www.movies.yahoo.com/blogs/movie-talk/alfred-hitchcock-creepy-infatuation-lea-+ding-ladies-195816079.html

[23] http://www.omg-facts.com/Science/Melanesians-Are-The-Only-Dark-Skinned-Pe/51251#la9WzTqibff6Y4wz.99

[24] http://www.genecards.org/cgi-bin/carddisp.pl?gene=TYRP1

[25] http://blogs.discovermagazine.com/gnxp/2012/05/case-closed-blonde-melanesians-understood/#.USJ5sKU4uVU

[26] http://papers.ssrn.com/sol3/papers.cfm?abstract_id=1859662

[27] Black Woman Fired From Hooters Because of Blonde Highlights -

http://www.huffingtonpost.com/2013/10/22/farryn-johnson-fired-hooters-blond-highlights-_n_4142108.html

[28] Multi-level marketing is a marketing strategy in which the sales force is compensated not only for sales they personally generate, but also for the sales of the other salespeople that they recruit. This recruited sales force is referred to as the participant's "downline", and can provide multiple levels of compensation.

[29] The Santa Clara Vanguard Drum and Bugle Corps (also known as "SCV", "Vanguard", or just "Santa Clara") is a World Class *(formerly Division I)* competitive junior drum and bugle corps. Based in Santa Clara, CA, the Santa Clara Vanguard is one of the thirteen founding member corps of Drum Corps International (DCI) and is a six-time DCI World Champion.

[30] Unity of Washington, DC is a center for spiritual growth and dynamic transformation, where people discover the joy of living, loving and serving through the understanding and application of the Spiritual Principles of Truth. Located at 1225 R Street NW, Washington, DC 20009.

[31] The Fashion Centre at Pentagon City, also known as Pentagon City Mall is an upscale shopping mall in Arlington, VA.

[32] One of London's most famous institutions for Afternoon Tea.

[33] The William Rumsey Aquatics Center is located in DC's exciting Eastern Market neighborhood. In the shadow of Capitol Hill, this aquatics center offers an 8 lane 20 yard x 25 yard pool, men and women locker rooms, wading pool, community room, and much more. Located at 635 North Carolina Avenue SE.

[34] Eastern Market, Washington DC's original and premier food & arts market. Located in the heart of the historic Capitol Hill neighborhood. Eastern Market is DC's destination for fresh food, community events, and on weekends, local farm-fresh produce and handmade arts and crafts. Located at 225 7th Street SE, Washington, DC 20003.

[35] Potomac Gardens, known to some of its residents as **"The Gardens"**, is a housing project located at 1225 G Street SE, in Capitol Hill, Southeast, Washington, D.C., thirteen blocks to the southeast of the United States Capitol building. The property is owned by the District of Columbia Housing Authority, and its 352-units are divided into family and senior housing. It was constructed between 1965 and 1968. In November 1967, the first families began moving in.

[36] Cleveland Park is a residential neighborhood in the Northwest quadrant of Washington, DC It is bounded by Rock Creek Park to the east, Wisconsin and Idaho Avenues to the west, Klingle and Woodley Roads to the south, and Rodman and Tilden Streets to the north. Its main commercial corridor lies along Connecticut Avenue, NW, where the eponymous Cleveland Park Station of the Washington Metro's Red Line can be found; another commercial corridor lies along Wisconsin Avenue. The neighborhood is known for its many late 19th century homes and the historic Art Deco Uptown Theater. It is also home to the William L. Slayton House and the Park and Shop, built in 1930, and one of the earliest strip malls..

[37] Metro Weekly is a free weekly magazine for the lesbian, gay, bisexual and transgender (LGBT) community in Washington, D.C., U.S.A. It was first published on May 5, 1994. Metro Weekly includes national and local news, interviews with LGBT leaders and politicians, community

event calendars, nightlife guides, and reviews of the District's arts and entertainment scene.

[38] LOL is an acronym for laughing out loud.

[39] Margaret Murray Washington School, also known as the M.M. Washington Career High School is a historic structure located in the Truston Circle neighborhood of Washington, DC. The curriculum provided "manual training for boys and domestic science and art for girls." Nursing was added during World War II and it was accredited afterwards. The school offered instruction to students at area elementary schools as well as high-school-age students who made up its student body.

[40] Medicaid in the United States is a social health care program for families and individuals with low income and resources. The Health Insurance Association of America describes Medicaid as a "government insurance program for persons of all ages whose income and resources are insufficient to pay for health care.

[41] Medicare is a national social insurance program, administered by the U.S. federal government since 1966, that guarantees access to health insurance for Americans aged 65 and older who have worked and paid into the system, and younger people with disabilities as well as people with end stage renal disease (Medicare.gov, 2012) and persons with amyotrophic lateral sclerosis. As a social insurance program, Medicare spreads the financial risk associated with illness across society to protect everyone, and thus has a somewhat different social role from for-profit private insurers, which manage their risk portfolio by adjusting their pricing according to perceived risk.

[42] In health insurance in the United States, a preferred provider organization (or PPO, sometimes referred to as

a participating provider organization or preferred provider option) is a managed care organization of medical doctors, hospitals, and other health care providers who have agreed with an insurer or a third-party administrator to provide health care at reduced rates to the insurer's or administrator's clients.

[43] Child Protective Services is the governmental agency in many states of the US that responds to reports of child abuse and neglect.

[44] Washington Lee High School (often simply called "W-L") is one of three traditional public high schools in the Arlington Public Schools district in Arlington, Virginia, covering grades 9-12. As of 2011, the school had over 2,000 students and 120 teachers. In 2010, W-L was listed at # 63 in Newsweek's listing of "America's Best High Schools," and # 3 in the state of Virginia..

[45] www.roboticmindsclothing.com

[46] http://icanshine.org/

[47] Adams Morgan is a culturally diverse neighborhood in Northwest Washington, DC, centered at the intersection of 18th Street and Columbia Road. Adams Morgan is considered the center of Washington's Hispanic immigrant community, and is a major night life area with many bars and restaurants, particularly along 18th Street (the primary commercial district) and Columbia Road. Much of the neighborhood is composed of 19th- and early 20th-century row houses and apartment buildings.

[48] Griffith Stadium was a sports stadium that stood in Washington, DC from 1911 to 1965, between Georgia Avenue and 5th Street, and between W Street and Florida Avenue NW. An earlier wooden baseball park had been built on the same site in 1891. It was called Boundary

Field or National Park, as its occupants were then known primarily by the nickname Nationals. This park was destroyed by a fire in March 1911 and replaced by a steel and concrete structure, also at first called National Park; it was renamed for Washington Senators owner Clark Griffith in 1920. The stadium was home to the American League Senators from 1911 through 1960, and to an expansion team of the same name for their first season in 1961. The venue hosted the 1937 and 1956 Major League Baseball All-Star Games as well as games of the 1924, 1925, and 1933 World Series. It served as home for the Negro League Homestead Grays during the 1940s. It was also home to the Washington Redskins of the National Footbal League for 24 seasons, from the time they transferred from Boston in 1937 through the 1960 season.

[49] Alpha Kappa Alpha (AKA) is the first Greek-lettered sorority established and incorporated by African-American college women. Membership is primarily for college educated women, but not all members have attended college. The sorority was founded on January 15, 1908, at Howard University in Washington, DC by a group of twenty students, led by Ethel Hedgeman Lyle.

[50] Bolling Air Force Base was a United States Air Force base in Washington, DC. In 2010 it was merged with Naval Support Facility Anacostia to form Joint Base Anacostia-Bolling.

[51] Frankie retired from the Department of Commerce September 31, 1995.

[52] The Verizon Center, formerly known as the MCI Center, is a sports and entertainment arena in Washinton, DC.

[53] The Red Hat Society (RHS) is a social organization

originally founded in 1998 in the United States for women age 50 and beyond, but now open to women of all ages. As of 2011, there were over 40,000 chapters in the United States and 30 other countries.

[54] Sunfest is the most popular festival of Ocean City. It celebrates the end of summer and the fabulous beginning of fall at the Ocean City Inlet and beach.

[55] www.sisterlocks.com

[56] Daisaku Ikeda (池田 大作, Ikeda Daisaku, born January 2, 1928, Japan) is president of Sōka Gakkai International (SGI), a Nichiren Buddhist lay association.

[57] http://www.beyondblackwhite.com/white-model-black-face-or-black-body-fashion-statement/

[58] http://www.wilhelminaphiladelphia.com/models/

[59] House of Cards is an American political drama television series, developed and produced by Beau Willimon. Available on Netflix.

[60] www.bechicimagez.com

www.ingramcontent.com/pod-product-compliance
Lightning Source LLC
Chambersburg PA
CBHW060904280326
41934CB00007B/1177